COLOR THERAPY IN A NUTSHELL

DR. JAGADEESH PILLAI

Made with ♥ on the Notion Press Platform
www.notionpress.com

This book is dedicated to the people who love colors and would like to heal with colors.

Contents

Contents

Prayer

Ganga tharanga ramaneeya jata kalapam,
Gowri niranthara vibhooshitha vama bhagam,
Narayana priya mananga madapaharam,
Varanasi pura pathim Bhajha Viswanatham ||

About The Author

Dr. Jagadeesh Pillai four times Guinness World Record holder, a voracious reader, writer, and true research scholar was born in Varanasi, the abode of Lord Shiva. He is Ph.D. in Vedic Science. He is a multi-faceted polymath with innate qualities, creative ideas and many remarkable achievements. Although his roots extend back to "Gods own Country"(Kerala), the residents of Varanasi feel proud of him and adore him as a child of Varanasi who caters to every individual in need without any expectations. A deep study into his profile reflects that he has added so many feathers to his cap which makes him quite unique. He is a four times Guinness Book of World Records Holder in the following subjects :

1. "Script to Screen" which he achieved by producing and directing a state of art animation film within the shortest time possible by breaking the earlier set record by Canadians. There are many national and international Awards and Recognitions to his credit.

2. Longest Line of Post Cards which he has done on the occasion of 163 years of Indian Postal Day by 16300 post cards. The event was also connected with a questionnaire about Indian Flag.

3. Largest Poster Awareness Campaign – This was achieved by designing an awareness campaign on the subject "Beti Bachao – Beti Padhao".

4. Largest Envelop – Towards tribute to Prime Minister's

initiative 'Make in India' – he has created about 4000 sq meter envelop using waste papers.

5. Attempted by lighting 70000 candles on a 210 kg cake to celebrate the 70th Indian Independence day recorded in World Records India.

6. Attempted a documentary on Dhamek Stupa of Sarnath dubbing in 17 languages, result is waiting from Guinness World Records.

He is versatile in Gita teaching. The young generation is fond of his Gita teaching and he has changed the life of many young through his continued motivational boost up and teachings.

He has composed and sung Gayatri Mantra in 1000 different tunes.

He has composed and sung Hanuman Chalisa in 108 different tunes.

He has composed and sung hundreds of Sanskrit Bhajans, Patriotic songs, etc.

He has written and directed so many short films and documentaries for awareness campaigns.

He has done voluntary services to UP Police and Kerala Police to spread awareness campaigns on the various issue through videos and photography.

He is on the path of authoring thousands of books on Indian culture, Indian Temples, and the life of extraordinary people.

It is hard to believe that he has produced and directed more than 100 Documentaries on a particular city (Varanasi) which is done by a single person.

He has helped and guided more than 25 boys and girls to achieve world records through various creative and innovative methods.

A multifaceted person who can apply the best of his intellect using the God-given blessings which have been showered upon every human being granting them an immense capacity to learn, experience, and experiment with many things and do wonders in this world of discrimination and disparities.

He is a teacher and a student at the same time who always learns every day and teaches every day. As a master, his weakness was that he never sticks to a particular subject. Perhaps this weakness gives him the strength to master any area which he came across.

Each of his days dawned with learning a new topic and he spend most of his time experimenting and researching it.

He is also a selfless social activist and a motivational speaker.

His life was full of struggle, ups and downs, and failures.

But he never gave up and faced all his trials and tribulations full of confidence. Today he is a successful young man with a lot of enthusiasm and rich life experience.

He has sung full Ram Charita Manas 51 hours audio by his own composition. He has also sung the whole Bhagavad-Gita in his own composition with a rhythmic background.

He has also sung "Lokah Samastha Sukhino Bhavantu" in 50 different languages.

Currently working on a detailed and scientific study on Veda, Upanishad, Puranas, Bhagavad Gita, etc.

He has composed and sung Hanuman Chalisa in 108 different compositions and Gayatri Mantra in 1008 different compositions.

Awards

Four Times Guinness World Records

Winner of Mahatma Gandhi Vishwa Shanti Puraskar

Mahatma Gandhi Global Peace Ambassador

Kashi Ratna Award

Dr. APJ Abdul Kalam Motivational Person of the Year 2017

Mother Teresa Award

Indira Gandhi Priyadarshini Award

Bharat Vikas Ratna Award

Udyog Ratna Award

Vigyan Prasar Award

Poorvanchal Ratn Samman

Preface

Color Therapy in a Nutshell

The fascinating world of color has a long history of use in therapies and treatments. Referred to as Chromotherapy, this practice relies on specific colors to influence how we feel and how we react in our daily lives. The theory is that different colors send out specific vibrations which can help with physical, mental, and emotional issues. From comforting blues for calmness, energizing pinks for joy, or grounding earth tones for stability - saturation & combination play a role within the healing power of color. Often products such as light sources, clothing palettes and paint are used strategically to access this form of therapy for its desired effect; results range from stress relief to improved sleep quality to bringing back balance into our lives.

Colors are an integral part of our lives; we cannot imagine a world without them. Color has a profound influence on our physical and mental wellbeing. At times, it can even act as a form of therapy. Here, I have summarized my notes on color therapy.

CHAPTER ONE

COLOR THERAPY

Colour therapy, also known as chromotherapy, is a type of alternative medicine that makes use of different colours of light to help create a balance among the physical, mental, emotional, and spiritual aspects of human life. This therapy works by stimulating the cells in the body that are responsible for providing energy and healing. The colours used in colour therapy are said to be able to have different effects on the mind and body; some of the types of colours commonly used in colour therapy include red, blue, green, purple, yellow, and orange.

The way that colour therapy works is that each colour is believed to stimulate certain areas of the brain, as well as the body's energies. By stimulating these areas, the colour therapy is said to improve overall health and wellbeing. Red is considered to be a stimulating colour and is associated with physical energy. Blue is associated with healing, and is said to help with calming and rejuvenation. Green is associated with love, gentleness, and relaxation. Yellow is associated with energy and focus, while purple is associated with wisdom and spiritual healing. Orange is associated with strength and endurance.

When engaging in this therapy, it is important to keep in mind that each colour has a different effect on individuals. While some people may find that they experience a calming effect from being exposed to certain colours, while others may experience an increase in energy and alertness. Additionally, different colours can have different effects on different parts of the body. For example, red light may help to reduce inflammation, while blue light may help to accelerate tissue repair.

Colour therapy may be used in a variety of ways. It may be used in a combination of the above mentioned colours in order to target specific areas of the body and maximize their healing potential. Additionally, colour therapy may be used to aid in mental and emotional healing, such as reducing anxiety and depression. Finally, colour therapy may be used to create a comfortable and relaxed environment in which people can take part in therapeutic activities.

Overall, colour therapy is a great way to help create a sense of balance in the mind and body. By stimulating the body's energies and manipulating the flow of energy, colour therapy can provide tremendous benefits to individuals looking to maintain or improve their overall wellbeing. While it is important to note that the effects of colour therapy may vary from person to person, it is still a valuable resource for creating a more harmonious and healthy life.

CHAPTER TWO

MOOD-BOOSTING BENEFITS OF COLOR THERAPY

Color Therapy is an alternative healing modality many people use to improve their mood. By utilizing the power of colors, it helps amplify the healing effects of light, which is why it often referred to as chromotherapy.

The concept of chromotherapy was first introduced in ancient India, with Ayurvedic medicines utilizing gemstones and colors to heal the body and mind. From there, the idea of using colors to boost one's mood spread throughout other parts of Asia, Europe, and across the world.

The way color therapy works is quite simple, but highly effective. Different colors can have a range of effects on the mind and body, and the colors are believed to stimulate energy channels in the body. For example, red is known to be energizing, blue promotes calming effects and relaxation, while yellow is uplifting. Therefore, when you look at colors, or use colors in your environment, they can alter your vibrations, emotions and thoughts, which can result in a better mood.

One of the most common ways people use color therapy to boost their moods is through visualizing colors. By picturing colors and allowing the colors to fill your mind and your body, you can energetically boost your mood. Practitioners may assign a specific color to specific emotional experiences they want to target, such as blue for sadness, yellow for joy, or green for peace. This can be helpful, as it uses colors to push emotional energy to the surface, enabling people to work through their feelings and eventually, letting go.

A second way people use colors to boost their mood is by using them in the physical environment. By using colors in your home decor, clothing pieces and artworks, you can subconsciously lift your spirits when you see them every day, enabling your mood to stay positive. Using a dimmer color palette in your surroundings, such as calm blue and green hues, can be both refreshing and relaxing. But don't be afraid to mix bolder colors as well, like purple, pink and yellow - these colors can give you an energy boost and help lift your mood.

In conclusion, color therapy can provide many mood boosting benefits. By using colors in visualizations, as well as in your environment, you can supercharge your mood and enjoy its numerous positive impacts, such as improved energy and awareness, improved mood regulation, along with a healthier and more optimistic outlook on life. So why not give it a try?

CHAPTER THREE

COLOUR THERAPY - VARIOUS METHODS AND COLOURS

Colour therapy, also known as chromotherapy, is a centuries-old healing technique that utilizes the power of colour to achieve its healing properties. This healing modality often involves a spectrum of colours in the form of light, art and natural materials, such as plants and stones, to facilitate healing and create balance within the body.

Colour therapy is based on the idea that each colour has unique energetic qualities, and when properly harnessed, can help provide relief from physical and psychological ailments. It is believed that when certain colours are viewed, used, or consumed, they will have an effect on the body, which can invoke certain emotions, improve one's mood, and build a greater sense of energy, clarity and balance. This practice is especially helpful for those who find a treatment that is non-medical, non-invasive and easily accessible.

The various methods for implementing colour therapy can be broken down into four categories: visual techniques, tactile methods, olfactory techniques, and ingestion.

The most common form of visual methods of colour therapy use light. This can be done through devices such as lamps and colored glass capsules which allow the color of light to be concentrated and moved throughout the body. This can improve overall mental and physical balance, helping with pain relief and stimulating creativity and relaxation.

The second visual technique used in color therapy is closely related to light therapy and works off of a similar principle: that the colors and their potency can be used to affect the body and psyche. Through art, the colors can be absorbed differently than the eye, to gain an even deeper level of healing. Through this method, colors can be used in paintings, sketches, jewelry and other artistic phenomena.

Moving on to more tactile methods, colour therapy is divided into two categories: contact with colors through objects and massage. Objects such as plants, stones, fabrics and crystals can be used to affect the body on a physical level by coming into direct contact. A massage with available colored oils and lotions can be used in the same way to relax, energize, and improve the health of the body.

The third and fourth categories of colour therapy are olfactory and ingestion methods. Olfactory treatment utilizes essential oils and incense, which when inhaled, allow the colors to interact with the limbic system to calm or energize. Ingestion treatments are typically done when an individual consumes certain colored foods and drinks. Through this method, colors can have a direct impact on the physical body, aiding in healing and providing pain relief.

Overall, colour therapy is an ancient healing technique that has stood the test of time for centuries. By harnessing the power of color and making it available to us through light, art, objects, massage, essential oils and nutrition, it demonstrates how powerful, and effective it can be. Whether it be working through physical pain, emotions, mental health issues, or simply as an aid.

CHAPTER FOUR

IMPORTANCE OF COLOURS IN OUR DAY TO DAY LIFE

Colours play an important role in our daily lives. For instance, they can influence our mood, create a certain atmosphere and convey a particular meaning, message or emotion. They are also used in communications and can be effective in brand recognition and advertising. Beyond these instances of visual communication, colours also help us to understand the world around us.

On first glance, colours may seem like an insignificant component of our everyday lives. After all, if everything was black and white, would anything really change? The answer is yes. Our human experience is dependent on colours and without them, our perception of the world would drastically change.

Colours can be used to trigger physiological reactions in humans. It can cause us to relax or become alert and energized. For instance, red is typically associated with danger and can increase the heart rate. This colour can be used in various industries, such as construction or even manufacturing, to alert employees of potential risks. Similarly, blue can help us to relax, reduce stress and make us feel more peaceful.

Colours can also be used to identify objects and make them easier to recognize. For example, traffic lights commonly use red, yellow, and green to distinguish between when it is safe to cross the street, when to proceed with caution, and when it is safe to continue. The colours are so familiar that they don't require any explanation and can be easily recognized, even if a person doesn't speak the same language. Furthermore, colours can be used to differentiate between emotions. For instance, blue can represent sadness while yellow can represent happiness.

Colours also create an aesthetic sense in our daily lives. They can be used to create interesting decor, express personal style and even improve the appearance of our living space. We may even choose to paint or decorate our home based on our mood or personal preference.

In conclusion, colours play a much larger role in our lives than most people realize. They are responsible for communicating and conveying messages, triggering physiological reactions, identifying objects and emotions, and creating an aesthetic sense in our everyday lives. Proper use of colours can make a major difference in our perception of the world.

CHAPTER FIVE

WHAT COLORS ARE BEST FOR DEPRESSION?

Depression is a widespread mental health issue that affects people of all ages. Many studies have been conducted to explore the role of color in combating depression. This phenomenon is known as color psychology and it involves the use of certain shades to evoke certain emotional responses in people. According to some studies, particular colors can help to reduce depression, anxiety, or stress. In this essay, we will explore which colors are best for depression.

The color most often associated with depression is blue. According to studies, blue has a calming effect on the mind and can help to relieve depression-related symptoms such as stress and anxiety. It is thought that blue has the power to reduce activity levels in the autonomic nervous system, leading to feelings of relaxation and improved emotional balance. Blue is also thought to be the best color for creating an atmosphere that is conducive to rest and sleep, which is an essential factor in the management of depression.

Green is another color that has been studied and found to be beneficial in the treatment of depression. Green has been found to be emotionally nurturing and helps to alleviate stress, anxiety, and sadness. Green also symbolizes hope, growth, and mental and emotional balance. It is believed that green can improve mental clarity and reduce fatigue, both of which are important in managing depression.

Orange is another encouraging color that has been recognized for its ability to combat depression. Orange is known to evoke an emotional response that helps people to remain optimistic and makes them feel more at ease. Additionally, orange can increase energy levels and help to boost mood and alertness. This can be especially helpful during times of depression when energy levels tend to be low.

Finally, yellow is another color that has been found to have a positive effect on mental health issues such as depression. It is known to inspire enthusiasm and optimism, helping to maintain a positive outlook. The warm and cheerful nature of yellow can help to lift the spirits and create a sense of emotional balance.

In conclusion, each individual responds differently to specific colors and what works for one person might not work for another. However, studies have found that blue, green, orange, and yellow are the four colors that have the most positive effect on depression. It is important to note that incorporating these colors into one's lifestyle is not a cure for depression and should be used in combination with conventional treatments in order to achieve the best results.

CHAPTER SIX

WHAT COLOURS HELP MENTAL HEALTH?

Colours have been found to influence a person's mental health in a powerful way. For centuries, colours have been associated with different moods and characteristics, and the power of colour has been used to help people with mental health issues. Certain colours appear to stimulate the senses, evoke calming or soothing effects and promote emotional balance.

Research has been carried out to determine the positive impact colours can have on mental health. Studies have found that certain colours affect moods, behaviour and emotional responses, with some resulting in physiological changes. It is believed that colours can affect areas of the brain, such as the hypothalamus, that are responsible for emotional regulation. By understanding the therapeutic and psychological effects of colour, we can improve the wellbeing of people struggling with mental health issues.

Warmer hues, such as yellow, orange and red, have been associated with stimulating effects. These colours can be used to brighten the atmosphere and alleviate feelings of sadness or depression. Yellow is known to stimulate physical as well as mental processes, making it a great choice for studying or working on complex tasks. Although yellow is associated with warmth and happy emotions, it can give off a feeling of unease when used in too much abundance.

On the other hand, cooler hues, such as blue, purple and green, have been linked to more calming effects. These shades evoke feelings of peacefulness and tranquillity, which can help those with anxiety or stress-related conditions. Blue, in particular, has been found to exert an influence strong enough to lower a person's heart rate and blood pressure. Green also has a calming and soothing effect, as it increases harmony and balance.

White, grey and black are seen as neutral tones, as each can range from being uplifting to dark and dreary. Generally, these colours are used to create a calming atmosphere. White promotes feelings of clarity and freshness, while black is commonly used to provide a sense of security and serenity. Grey is often used to create a mellow atmosphere, while providing contrast and depth.

The power of colour when it comes to improving mental health should never be underestimated. By understanding the psychological and physiological effects of various hues, we can create environments that are more conducive to wellbeing and emotional balance. By exploring the effects of different colours and experimenting, people can find a palette that works for them and helps to restore their mental wellbeing.

Colours have been found to influence a person's mental health in a powerful way. For centuries, colours have been associated with different moods and characteristics, and the power of colour has been used to help people with mental health issues. Certain colours appear to stimulate the senses, evoke calming or soothing effects and promote emotional balance.

Research has been carried out to determine the positive impact colours can have on mental health. Studies have found that certain colours affect moods, behaviour and emotional responses, with some resulting in physiological changes. It is believed that colours can affect areas of the brain, such as the hypothalamus, that are responsible for emotional regulation. By understanding the therapeutic and psychological effects of colour, we can improve the wellbeing of people struggling with mental health issues.

Warmer hues, such as yellow, orange and red, have been associated with stimulating effects. These colours can be used to brighten the atmosphere and alleviate feelings of sadness or depression. Yellow is known to stimulate physical as well as mental processes, making it a great choice for studying or working on complex tasks. Although yellow is associated with warmth and happy emotions, it can give off a feeling of unease when used in too much abundance.

On the other hand, cooler hues, such as blue, purple and green, have been linked to more calming effects. These shades evoke feelings of peacefulness and tranquillity, which can help those with anxiety or stress-related conditions. Blue, in particular, has been found to exert an influence strong enough to lower a person's heart rate and blood pressure. Green also has a calming and soothing effect, as it increases harmony and balance.

White, grey and black are seen as neutral tones, as each can range from being uplifting to dark and dreary. Generally, these colours are used to create a calming atmosphere. White promotes feelings of clarity and freshness, while black is commonly used to provide a sense of security and serenity. Grey is often used to create a mellow atmosphere, while providing contrast and depth.

The power of colour when it comes to improving mental health should never be underestimated. By understanding the psychological and physiological effects of various hues, we can create environments that are more conducive to wellbeing and emotional balance. By exploring the effects of different colours and experimenting, people can find a palette that works for them and helps to restore their mental wellbeing.

CHAPTER SEVEN

WHAT COLOR CAUSES ANXIETY

If there is one color that can cause anxiety, it is most certainly red. Red is said to stimulate the senses and increase heart rate. This is because of its connection to danger and danger signals, such as a stop sign or a firetruck. Even seeing the color red from a distance will elevate a person's stress levels and cause a feeling of disorientation.

In order to better understand the relationship between the color red and anxiety, it is important to understand that colors can influence one's physiological and psychological states. Red stands out more than other colors, so when it is present in a room it can raise your blood pressure, heart rate, and breathing rate. Red can also lead to feelings of anger and agitation which are usually associated with anxiety.

So how can color therapy help with anxiety brought on by red? Color therapy is a form of energy healing that uses the power of color to evoke an energetic shift. By projecting certain colors onto the body, their healing power can balance one's physical and emotional state.

Since the color red is associated with fear, color therapists might suggest calm and soothing colors such as blues, greens, and purples. These hues, which represent tranquility and relaxation, can be used to balance out the disturbing effects of the color red. For example, a warm blue or green color can bring in an inviting hue and instant calming effect which in turn can reduce levels of anxiety.

Furthermore, color therapy can help bring about physical, mental, and emotional balance without the use of medications or other more invasive forms of treatment. This cost and time efficient approach to balancing the energy system can provide great relief and support to individuals struggling with anxiety related issues.

In conclusion, red is the color that most often causes feelings of anxiety, and color therapy can be a great resource in healing this fear. By introducing calming and harmonizing hues, color therapy can be a useful tool in providing balance and comfort from the overwhelming feeling of fear.

Color and trait anxiety are two related yet distinct factors that can significantly impact an individual's level of state anxiety. State anxiety is an intense feeling of apprehension, fear, or worry that is associated with an imminent or anticipated event. Color and trait anxiety can influence an individual's perception of their own level of state anxiety. This essay will explore the effects of color and trait anxiety on state anxiety, including the role of the environment, individual judgement, and the body's natural physiological response.

It is believed that color has a powerful influence on our emotions and can strongly influence an individual's level of state anxiety. Visual stimuli such as color cues in an environment can trigger a response in the body, helping to create and amplify an individual's experience of state anxiety. This is especially evident in surroundings that trigger negative and unsettling feelings, such as a hospital or courtroom. Furthermore, certain colors can have associations with certain negative emotions, creating a stimulus-response mechanism which heightens a person's experience of state anxiety.

Trait anxiety, or an individual's predisposition to experience anxious thoughts and feelings, is another factor that influences an individual's state anxiety. It has been suggested that trait anxiety can be a determining factor in creating a level of uncertainty and apprehension, in both anticipated and current events, creating a heightened sense of state anxiety. Recent research has supported the claim that trait anxiety interacts with other environmental and psychological factors to create a heightened level of state anxiety.

Not only do color and trait anxiety influence the mental experience of state anxiety, but they also have a physical effect. An individual's fight-or-flight response is activated in the presence of both color and trait anxiety, triggering a cascade of physical changes such as an increase in pulse rate, elevated blood pressure, and the release of hormones. These physical reactions to both color and trait anxiety create an individualized experience of state anxiety.

In conclusion, the effects of color and trait anxiety on state anxiety cannot be overstated. Color cues in an environment and an individual's innate predisposition to anxious thoughts and feelings work together to create a heightened experience of state anxiety. Furthermore, the physical effects of color and trait anxiety create a personalized experience of anxious feelings. It is therefore important to be mindful of the role of color and trait anxiety in our lives and take measures to reduce their influence on our levels of state anxiety.

CHAPTER EIGHT

WHAT COLOR CALMS OUR MIND

It is a widely accepted notion that colors have a great influence on our minds and emotions. For example, certain colors have a calming effect, while others can increase energy or irritate and agitate the mind. In the realm of color therapy, or chromotherapy, it has been observed that colors have powerful psychological effects which can help to soothe, relax, and improve overall health.

The color which best soothes and calms me is blue. Personally, I find blue possesses a calming, tranquil quality. Whenever I am feeling overwhelmed or agitated, blue can work as an anchor to help me to relax and recenter myself. It is widely accepted that blue is the most calming of colors, and can help to reduce anxiety, stress, and tension. Those seeking to calm their mood can try decorating the living spaces with blue furniture and decorations, or even just add a few blue accessories.

In color therapy, blue is said to have a beneficial effect on the emotional and physical state of the body, which can help to reduce stress, reduce fatigue, and nurture the mind and body. Blue also possesses emotional healing qualities, which can have a beneficial effect on the nervous system. When it comes to emotional healing, blue can help to dispel anger and other negative emotions, allowing a feeling of serenity and peace to take their place.

The science behind blue's calming effects lies in its psychological properties. Blue is associated with a feeling of security and safety, which can be helpful for people suffering from anxiety or phobias. It can also tap into a more spiritual place, helping to open channels of deeper understanding and quiet awareness. Blue is also believed to promote logical thinking, mental clarity, and positive communication, which can be helpful to those seeking to better understand their minds.

Overall, blue is a powerful hue which can greatly help to soothe and calm the mind. For those looking to relax, let go, and bring balance to their emotions, blue can be an invaluable color. By applying its calming effects to the physical and emotional state of the body, blue can help offer relief and healing to those struggling with exhaustion, anxiety, and agitation.

CHAPTER NINE

COLOURS & POSITIVE ENERGY

When looking to achieve a sense of happiness, many people turn to color. Colors can evoke powerful emotions, and these emotions can affect our moods and our outlook on life, in both positive and negative ways. Colors can help to create a sense of peace and balance, invoke a feeling of invigoration and positivity, or generate a feeling of serenity and relaxation. By understanding the symbolism behind each color, we can begin to create an atmosphere that will help to foster positive energy and promote good vibes.

Yellow is seen as a color of sunshine, happiness and optimism. Its bright and warm qualities can help to foster feelings of confidence, hope, and positivity. This color radiates energy, enthusiasm, and joy, making it great for a home office or work space. Research has also shown that yellow can help to stimulate creativity, concentration, and communication. It can also help to brighten up any room and make people more optimistic.

Green also represents renewal, growth, and rejuvenation. It is strongly linked to nature, bringing us a sense of calmness, balance and peace. It can be very helpful in reducing stress and anxiety, and promoting relaxation. This cool and calming color is great for any space, particularly for those looking for a relaxing environment.

Shades of blue can generate a sense of harmony, honesty and understanding. This gentle, yet dynamic color invokes a feeling of trust and loyalty. As it has traditionally been associated with the calming waters of the sea, blue can be a great addition to any room if you are looking to create a sense of peace and serenity. It also can aid in concentration, making it a great color for learning spaces, such as classrooms and study areas.

Orange is a dynamic color that promotes energy, enthusiasm, and drive. It stimulates enthusiasm, ambition and creativity, making it a great choice of color to use in a work space or office. This bright, happy color can help to encourage productivity and positivity, and can help to boost self-esteem.

The bright and vibrant colors of yellow, green, blue, and orange can be used to create a positive atmosphere that will help to invigorate and energize us. By understanding the symbols and meanings associated with each color, we can use color to create the perfect atmosphere to promote feelings of positivity and good vibrations.

CHAPTER TEN

COLOR AND EMOTION

When we talk about the psychology of color, we often think of color as having an emotional component. While this is certainly true, it's important to understand that the emotional impact of color is highly subjective. Every person has their own unique experiences and worldview that shapes how they view and interact with the world around them. This means there can be no single emotion associated with any given color.

That said, there's no denying that certain hues have become associated with strong feelings and emotions. Most people agree that blue and purple are often seen as calming and relaxing colors, while yellow and orange are often seen as energizing and uplifting. Red is universally associated with strong emotions like anger, passion, or love. Moreover, it has been observed that specific shades or tones of a given color can have a stronger emotional impact than others. For instance, the cooler shades of blue often invoke a feeling of calm and serenity, while yellow in warmer hues can bring about a sense of joy and happiness.

Ultimately, when it comes to the most emotional color, it's hard to say. It depends entirely on the individual and their experiences. Though some might argue that red is the most powerful, others may find that a different hue is emotionally more significant. It could be blue for its calming effects, or even green for its association with growth and renewal. Ultimately, the emotional impact of color comes down to personal perception and how one chooses to express and interpret it.

There's no doubt that color plays an important role in our lives and can affect us emotionally in both positive and negative ways. It's important to be conscious of the colors we use and how they may impact our mood and emotions. Whether we use them to create balance or induce strong feelings, understanding the emotional power of color can help us to create the right atmosphere and tap into our feelings in a more profound way.

CHAPTER ELEVEN

NEGATIVE COLOURS

The most negative color, hands down, is black. It is associated with death, sadness, and something that casts a pallor of disappointment, fear and dread. It is often associated with mourning and unhappiness, as one might wear black to a funeral to show respect for and mourn the passing of a loved one. Black's connotations and associations have been around for centuries, in cultures all around the world, and it is universally seen as a color of gloom and sorrow.

Another powerful meaning of black is its association with evil, darkness and death—partly because it is the colour of the night sky and the veil of darkness that shrouds us when the sun sets. In older cultures, black was often seen to be the colour of mysteries, secrets and ignorance. It was also connected to shadow energy, and the symbolic of inner realms and invisible worlds. In some ancient societies, black was tied to malevolent forces, powers of sorcery and werewolves. As a result, many people see it as an ominous, sinister colour, which is reflected in cultures that embrace darker shades in artwork, films or music.

A darker shade of black has also come to represent

authority, power, and prestige. It is commonly associated with certain kinds of wealth and prosperity, as black is usually seen as an expensive, classier color than other colors. However, wearing black does come with a few downsides — for one thing, going for an all-black outfit can make one appear almost foreboding and intimidating, or at worst, dishonest.

Colors often affect us emotionally, and black is no exception. Its dark, ominous undertone can make a person feel pessimistic, exhausted, and low in mood. It can create a sense of hopelessness and sadness, and is often interpreted as a sign of fear and negative energy. People that are already struggling with depression could also find themselves becoming more affected by black, and it could be beneficial to them to stay away from wearing black or having it in their surroundings.

Finally, one should also be aware of how black can potentially influence the way others interpret us. From the landlord to the classmate, people may interpret our all-black wardrobe as a sign of aggressiveness, pessimism or mysterious tendencies. This could have negative implications on social life and one's relationships, business and job prospects.

Black is an incredibly powerful, symbolic color that has been woven into different cultures for centuries. However, interpreting it in a positive way is key, and being aware of the potential consequences that wearing black could have is also important. Despite its negativity and associations with darkness, black can also be very stylish, and with the right outfit, even something negative can be transformed into something beautiful.

CHAPTER TWELVE

COLOURS AND HOME

Colour therapy is a type of holistic healing that uses the energizing power of colours to improve physical and mental health. By introducing colour into a home environment, you can create a balanced and healthy atmosphere that promotes wellness and wellness.

When selecting a colour scheme for home, you should consider the colours associated with a therapeutic purpose. Certain colours are thought to have a calming effect, such as blues and greens. These hues are also believed to foster feelings of relaxation and contentment. Shades of yellow and orange are energizing and invigorating, perfect for areas of the home used for activity and creativity. For focus and concentration, blues and greens are often recommended since they are believed to reduce stress levels.

You may want to consider the tones and shades of colours you choose as well. For example, bright hues of yellow and orange can be overwhelming and should usually be used in moderation. On the other hand, gentle shades of warm colours like beige and pastels can be comforting. Additionally, it's wise to pay attention to the undertones of a colour; the bluer side of green is calming, while a yellowish-green is more invigorating.

In contrast to calming colours, vibrant colours are energizing and stimulating and can be used to brighten up an area or add some pizzazz. Reds, magentas, and hot pinks are passionate and passionate colours that bring excitement, add drama, and show enthusiasm. On the other hand, cooler hues of blues, purples, and greens can make rooms feel tranquil and inviting.

Finally, the use of white or neutral colours can be calming and reliable. These colours will help set the stage for the other shades by creating a backdrop and helping the other colours to pop. In all, the amount of colour as well as its tone and intensity should be thoughtfully considered when picking colour palettes for a home.

Overall, thoughtful colour selection can help to create a therapeutic environment in your home that assists in promoting emotional and mental health and wellbeing. By choosing the right hues, tones, and shades, you can promote relaxation, energy, focus, and enthusiasm. As with most things, it's important to experiment and find colours that work best in your space. Most of all, use colour to create a home atmosphere that nurtures your wellbeing.

CHAPTER THIRTEEN

SUCCESS AND ENCOURAGEEMENT

The color of success is not one single hue, but a kaleidoscope of bright, vibrant color. Success is achieved via hard work, dedication, and creativity, and this complex combination of ingredients can be represented in many different colors. Various shades of blue can indicate resilience and perseverance, while shades of green can represent growth and ambition. The warm and optimistic hues of yellow can celebrate accomplishments and highlight potential, while shades of red can signify passion and desire. The diversity of colors associated with success represents the scope and variety of achievements that can be accomplished with determination and dedication.

Each color has its own symbolism and as such, can be used to encourage success. As the shades of blue represent strength and resilience, they can be used to encourage individuals to take on difficult challenges and keep pushing forward. Reds and oranges indicate eagerness and action, so they can motivate individuals to take the first step towards achieving their goals. Greens and blues represent balance, growth, and harmony; these tones can be used to help focus and maintain an optimistic vision for the future. The array of colors associated with success can be used in combination to really emphasize the spirit of progress and personal achievement.

When used to promote and inspire success, color can help individuals recognize their goals and remind them of their purpose. Color can serve as a visual representation of success. For example, seeing a brilliant blue tone after reaching a long-term goal can bring a sense of accomplishment and appreciation of the hard work that was put in along the way. By surrounding oneself with energizing colors, individuals can be reminded that although hard work and dedication are required, success is ultimately possible and achievable.

In summary, the array of colors associated with success can offer a mood board of inspiration and motivation. Different shades give specific meanings to achievements and provide motivation to achieve more. This combination of symbolic and energetic hues can remind individuals of their goals and encourage them to stay focused on the path ahead. By understanding the power of color, individuals can empower themselves to reach their fullest potential and achieve success.

CHAPTER FOURTEEN

THE PSYCHOLOGY OF COLOR IN BUSINESS

Color is more than a simple form of communication and can have a powerful influence on our decisions, behavior, and perception. It can influence a customer's perception of a business and the choices we make when purchasing products and services. The psychology of color in business is an important element to consider when creating a brand identity.

Different colors evoke different emotions in people and can be used strategically to influence customer decisions. For example, red is often associated with power, passion, and energy; while blue is associated with feelings of trust, reliability and communication. When designing a brand identity, it is essential to consider the implications of specific colors in order to create a successful and effective message.

In the business world, color can also be used to

communicate status and power. For example, gold is often associated with wealth and prosperity, while silver is usually thought of as modern and sophisticated. A company might create a logo featuring warm gold tones to communicate that they are a successful business with plenty of resources to offer customers. Likewise, a company might utilize a more modern color palette featuring silver tones to communicate their innovative approach and current approach to their business.

Moreover, certain colors can also be used to influence customer perceptions and behaviors in a retail environment. For example, red is often used to draw attention to a particular product and encourage customers to make a purchase. On the other hand, blue is often used to create feelings of calm and serenity, which can be beneficial in creating a relaxed shopping environment.

In conclusion, the psychology of color in business is an essential element that should not be overlooked. Colors can be used strategically to influence customer perception, evoke certain emotions, and communicate brand status and power. It is important to consider the implications of specific colors when selecting a brand identity in order to ensure that the message is effective and successful.

CHAPTER FIFTEEN

HOW COLOR HELP HEAL PHYSIC AND MIND

The concept of incorporating color into healing is an ancient idea, with evidence showing that it can be traced back as far as the 4th century BCE. Since then, many cultures – including Indian and Chinese – have embraced the use of colored light and crystals to assist in the healing of both the physical and mental body.

On a physical level, each color has a specific energy, therapeutic effect and healing capacity. For example, red can be used to stimulate the body into a state of emergency response to prepare for an injury or illness. It can also be used to increase circulation, encourage the body to burn fat, boost the immune system and increase circulation to an area of injury.

On a mental level, colors can help us to connect with our emotions, create a sense of inner peace and tranquility, and even encourage acceptance of our current situation.

Blue, for example, is known as a calming color which has the ability to connect us to feeling of inner balance and relaxation. Brown, on the other hand, is known for its grounding effect, helping us to connect with our physical body and with the present moment.

Different colors also evoke different feelings, allowing us to access deeper emotions, and even providing access to spiritual qualities. While green is known to bring health and abundance, purple can help us to find joy, contentment and understanding. White, on the other hand, can help heal a feeling of separateness and open our hearts to an expansive state.

The healing power of colors goes hand in hand with the power of intention. Using color as part of healing, rather than just as adornment, is a way of setting an intention – of saying aloud what it is we want to achieve. Whether it's to reduce anxiety, to bring forth courage, to create balance or to promote healing, color can help lend support to our desired outcomes.

In conclusion, color plays a profound role in the healing of both the physical and mental body. By selecting the right colors, or combination of colors, we can tap into the healing power of the universe and manifest our desired outcomes. Whether it's for immediate relief, ongoing healing, or ongoing spiritual connection, color can be a powerful tool of transformation. Embracing the power of color and bringing it into our lives can be an incredibly enriching experience – one which has the capacity to change us and our circumstances for the better.

CHAPTER SIXTEEN

CHROMOTHERAPY AND ITS SCIENCE

Chromotherapy, also known as "color therapy," is an alternative, holistic therapy that uses light and color to balance bodily energies, both physical and emotional. Originating in ancient Egypt and the practices of various cultures, the theory is that different colors have the ability to influence a person's emotions, thoughts, and physical wellbeing. Chromotherapy is a non-invasive technique and there is no scientific evidence that supports it, yet it is growing in popularity as a complementary therapy.

Chromotherapy's core belief is that each color of the spectrum has its own vibratory energy, according to the Eastern Science of Color. Color vibrations are also used in Ayurvedic traditional medicines. The science of chromotherapy states that our bodies absorb light energy and this energy affects our emotional, mental, and physical wellbeing. Color therapy is based on the idea that color and light are transforming agents, which can help to restore balance to the body's energies.

Proponents of chromotherapy suggest that the vibrations

of different colors affect a person's life force energy, known as Qi in traditional Chinese medicine. Chromotherapy can be used in multiple ways, for example, by utilizing different shades of colored light, gemstones, paintings, clothing, and even aromas to manipulate one's energy. Practitioners of chromotherapy will utilize color to stimulate or suppress certain physical or emotional symptoms.

Many people who have used chromotherapy have experienced positive results; however, there is not sufficient scientific evidence to support the effectiveness of the therapy. More research is required to accurately assess the benefits of color therapy. Furthermore, chromotherapy practitioners should have extensive knowledge and experience in the therapy to deliver the right treatment. Before engaging in chromotherapy, it is important to consult a qualified professional for an accurate diagnosis of any medical condition and advice.

In conclusion, Chromotherapy does not have credible scientific evidence to back it up at this current time, but it still has many supporters and those who have claimed to experience positive effects from the therapy. Further research is needed to understand the mechanism of color therapy and its clinical effectiveness.

CHAPTER SEVENTEEN

WAYS TO IMPROVE YOUR LIFE WITH COLOURS

Color therapy is an alternative healing practice that uses different colors to produce healing effects. Colors reflect certain emotions and feelings and can be used to create balance, harmony and emotional and physical healing. Each color has a unique energy and vibration and can be used to create overall well-being in your life. Here are 20 ways you can use color therapy to improve your life.

1. Utilize a color wheel to help you balance your energy. You can use the wheel to identify which colors will work best to improve your emotional and physical health.

2. Surround yourself with colorful objects. Place colorful objects and artwork around your home and office to introduce positive energy into your environment.

3. Wear bright, vibrant colors. Wearing colorful clothing is a great way to enhance your life with color therapy.

4. Create a mood board. Make a mood board with pictures, quotes and color swatches to help unearth and bring forth positive emotions.

5. Place color charged items in your home. Place items such as leaves, candles, and incense in your home with colors that are linked to the emotions and feelings that you want to evoke.

6. Make your food colorful. Foods that are brightly colored can provide nutritional benefits as well as introduce beneficial energy into your body.

7. Dress your bed in color. Adorn your bed with brightly colored sheets and pillow cases to infuse your sleeping area with vibrant energy.

8. Express yourself with color. Use paints, colored pencils, and other art materials to express yourself through art and color.

9. Light up your living space. Place colored lights around your living space to introduce different hues and atmospheres.

10. Seek out inspiration in colored gems. Holding or wearing gemstones that are brightly colored can bring clarity and focus to your life.

11. Try color meditation. Sit in a peaceful place and focus on different colors. As you focus on each color, take deep breaths and allow yourself to fully embrace that color's

vibration.

12. Add color to your bath time. Adding bright chunks of colorful soap to your bath will help you to relax as well as to introduce helpful energies into your life.

13. Practice crystal color therapy. Place colorful crystals around your house to fill the area with calming energy.

14. Explore color psychology. Understand how certain colors affect your mood and use this knowledge to make color choices that promote harmony.

15. Get creative with color. Use color to give life to different projects such as painting, scrapbooking and other crafts to make your life more vivid.

16. Heal yourself with light. Practice chromotherapy by exposing yourself to light therapy in different colors to promote physical healing.

17. Use color to transform your environment. Place bright curtains in your living space to change the atmosphere and fill it with positive energy.

CHAPTER EIGHTEEN

COLOR PSYCHOLOGY FOR DRESS

Color psychology is the study of how colors impact our mood, behaviors, and thoughts. It's thought that certain colors are better suited to certain occasions, depending on the type of message you'd like to send or the desired outcome. In other words, the color you choose for what you wear can set the stage for a successful outcome, whether it be for a job interview, a first date, or a meeting with your boss.

Traditionally, black has been the color of authority and power. Depending on the context, it can also represent strength, elegance, or sophistication. It's often seen as an "all-around" safe color to wear as it rarely clashes with other colors. When it comes to job interviews, this may be a favorable color choice as it shows you're serious and ready to impress.

Another color known for conveying strength and power is blue. It often has a calming effect and is associated with trustworthiness. In a professional setting, it's great for creating a friendly and inviting atmosphere. Green, on the other hand, is known for its ability to convey balance and harmony; it's an excellent choice to create a relaxed and focused atmosphere.

Red and orange are highly visible colors and can be quite impactful. Both are associated with enthusiasm, confidence, and passion. As such, they tend to be great for dates or for introducing yourself in social situations. Red is particularly effective for grabbing someone's attention and giving off a seductive vibe.

Lastly, yellow is seen as a cheerful and optimistic color. It can be helpful in boosting your mood and giving off an inviting, carefree vibe. It's great for a bright first impression and can help create a positive atmosphere.

When choosing what to wear, it's important to consider the type of environment you'll be interacting in and the desired outcome. In general, black, blue, green, red, orange, and yellow are all great colors to consider, depending on the desired outcome. All these colors can convey a variety of messages, depending on the context and how they're paired with other colors. So think carefully before you choose your outfit and you'll be sure to set yourself up for success.

CHAPTER NINETEEN

IS COLOR THERAPY SCIENTIFICALLY PROVEN?

Color therapy, also known as chromotherapy, is a form of treatment that uses the visible spectrum of light and color to improve physical and mental health. Chromotherapy is rooted in the idea that color has an effect on the human body and psyche, dating back to the ancient cultures of Egypt, India, and Greece. Over the years, this practice has been used to treat a variety of ailments, from depression and anxiety to physical pain and even cancer.

Though it has been popular for thousands of years, it is only recently that color therapy has been investigated scientifically. One of the earliest studies on the potential effectiveness of chromotherapy was conducted by U.S. Naval Academy in 1964, which found that exposure to certain colors could lower blood pressure. Studies since then have investigated the effects of color for a variety of conditions, such as cancer, depression, and insomnia.

The most commonly studied component of color therapy has been its ability to affect mood and mental states. While the research in this field is still in its early stages, several studies have found that certain colors can have a positive effect on mood and emotion. For example, a study conducted by the University of Geneva in 2018 found that exposing participants to blue may reduce symptoms of stress and anxiety. Similarly, a study by the University of Granada in 2019 found that exposure to green can increase positive emotions and reduce negative ones.

Other research has looked into the physiological benefits of chromotherapy. For example, a 2016 study found that blue light can help to regulate circadian rhythms and improve sleep quality. Meanwhile, researchers at Harvard University found that exposure to green light helped to reduce inflammation, pain, and fatigue in people with chronic conditions.

Despite the potential benefits of chromotherapy, there is still a lack of conclusive evidence regarding its effectiveness. Many of the studies that have been conducted are of low quality, and more rigorous investigation is needed to determine the full extent of its benefits and determine the optimal doses and wavelengths of color to use. Additionally, it is important to consider the cultural and historical context of chromotherapy, as its effects may differ between individuals and cultures.

Overall, although some preliminary research has demonstrated positive results for color therapy, more rigorous research is needed to establish its effectiveness. Nonetheless, it is clear that color can have a powerful influence on physical and mental health, and it is certainly an avenue worth exploring for those seeking relief from an array of ailments.

CHAPTER TWENTY

IMPORTANCE OF COLOUR THERAPY

Color therapy is the practice of utilizing colors and light to promote healing, mental wellbeing, and soothing relaxation. Used for years in traditional remedies and complementary/alternative therapies, color therapy has been used to treat various physical, mental, and emotional issues. A recent study has found that people who regularly use color therapy have reported experiencing improved sleep, calmness, and better moods. This has prompted many medical professionals to start incorporating color therapy into their care plans for both physical and mental health issues.

The primary goal of color therapy is to promote relaxation, mental well-being, and healing. Colors surrounding us in daily life have the power to affect our emotions. Lighting can also be used to change the atmosphere in a room and the mood of an individual. Color therapy takes advantage of these qualities, targeting the emotions and energy levels to stimulate healing. This can be done through the use of crystals, gemstones, and other forms of light.

Color therapy works by targeting the chakras, which are the seven major energy centers in the body. Each color corresponds to one of the chakras, which are blue (throat area), yellow (solar plexus), green (heart), red (root area), purple (crown area), white (total balance), and orange (sacral area). When these colors are used in combination, they can bring balance and healing throughout the body.

Symptoms of physical and mental illnesses can also be relieved with color therapy. From depression to digestive problems, the power of color has been used to help people overcome their issues. For example, some studies have found that blue and green can be used to reduce feelings of anxiety and depression, as well as physical pain. Red has been used to energize and stimulate its user while yellow can aid digestion and improve focus. Even colors such as white, purple, and orange can be used to bring peace, clarity, and vitality.

Color therapy also enabled people to tap into their creative potential, enhancing their ability to develop emotionally and mentally. By using colors in different ways, individuals are able to increase their creativity and stimulate mental acuity. By using colors and light in a coordinated way, individuals can better manage their stress and emotions which can lead to improved self-confidence and better sense of self.

In conclusion, the importance of color therapy is clear: it helps to promote healing, mental wellbeing, and relaxation. By harnessing the power of colors, individuals are able to activate the chakras and balance their energies. It also handily relieves the symptoms of physical and mental illnesses as well as enhances creativity and increases one's overall sense of well-being. By understanding the power of color and light, we can learn to use these tools to take charge of our emotional and physical wellbeing.

CHAPTER TWENTY-ONE

SUMMARY

Color therapy, also known as chromotherapy, is an alternative medical technique used for wellness and healing. It is based on the use of colors and their electromagnetic wavelengths to restore balance in our lives and to bring about a sense of peace, calm and relaxation. This practice is believed to have been used since ancient times, and has been used in many cultures and countries to promote health and wellness.

The human body is able to absorb light and energy from colors that are both visible and invisible to us, and this energy is believed to have many beneficial effects on the body, including increased relaxation, pain relief, and emotional balance. Color therapy is based on the idea that each color vibrates at a different wavelength and frequency, which affects different parts of the body. For example, red is believed to increase circulation and provide energy, while blue has a calming and relaxing effect on the mind. Color also has an effect on the body's chakras, which are believed to be energy centers within the body that are connected to physical and emotional well-being.

In color therapy, different colors may be used to target

different areas for healing. For example, the use of green is believed to help restore balance to the heart chakra, while yellow is believed to bring cheerfulness and joy. Colors can also be used in combination to create a "color bath", in which colorful lights are placed around a person to focus on individual areas for healing. In addition, colored gemstones and crystals may also be used for healing purposes.

The importance of color therapy lies in its ability to restore balance in all areas of life. By targeting the chakras and the body's energy centers, color therapy can help balance physical, mental, emotional and spiritual health. It has been used to help reduce stress and anxiety, as well as to improve one's sleep, focus and productivity. All of these benefits can lead to a greater sense of well-being and overall improved quality of life.

In addition, color therapy can be used to enhance creativity, as it works to open and activate the higher centers of the brain. It can also be used to increase motivation and give people an overall feeling of positivity and satisfaction with life.

In summary, color therapy is a holistic wellness practice that has been used for centuries to promote relaxation, vitality, and a sense of overall well-being. By targeting the body's energy centers, it works to restore balance in mind, body and spirit, helping to reduce stress and anxiety, boost creativity, and improve a person's outlook on life.

Contact

9839093003

myrichindia@gmail.com

drjagadeeshpillai@facebook

jagadeeshpillai@youtube

www.JAGADEESHPILLAI.com

Printed by Libri Plureos GmbH in Hamburg,
Germany